# 50 Classic Cocktails

STEP-BY-STEP

# 50 Classic Cocktails

## Oona van den Berg

Photography by Steve Baxter

STRATHEARN BOOKS LIMITED
Toronto, Canada

Many thanks to alcohol aficionados:
Michael Fussell, James Fischer, Nicky Moores, Adrian Heath-Saunders.

First published in 1996 by Lorenz Books

This edition published by
STRATHEARN BOOKS LIMITED
Toronto, Canada

ISBN 1 85967 273 6

A CIP catalogue record is available from the British Library

*Publisher*: Joanna Lorenz
*Senior Cookery Editor*: Linda Fraser
*In-house Editor*: Maggie Mayhew
*Designer*: Eric Thompson
*Photographer*: Steve Baxter
*Stylist*: Judy Williams


PHOTOGRAPHIC CREDIT
Many thanks to Fiskars UK Ltd for the use of their range of Kitchen Devils knives and
chopping boards, to Magimix for use of the Professional blender and Privilege food
processor and to DuPont for the loan of the Berndes Signocast saucepans.

MEASURES
Three sets of equivalent measurements have been provided in these
recipes, in the following order:
Bar measures, metric and imperial. It is essential that units of measurements are not
mixed within each recipe. Where conversions result in awkward numbers, these have
been rounded for convenience, but are accurate enough to produce successful results.
Note: 1 measure = $\frac{1}{6}$ of a gill = 22.5ml

Printed and bound in Hong Kong

# CONTENTS

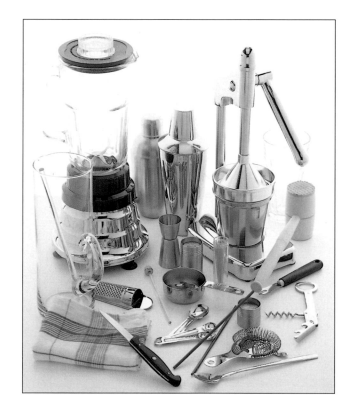

# INTRODUCTION

The true origin of the first cocktails is uncertain, but without doubt it was in America that these "mixed drinks" gained the greatest popularity and where many of the more recent cocktail bar favourites were concocted. Cocktails developed in America with bourbon, Southern Comfort and Canadian rye whisky vying for attention. Prohibition was intended to curb drinking habits but only resulted in people ingeniously distilling their own spirits, which were softened by the addition of mixers. From the late thirties and the forties the cocktail truly arrived in England. Chic and classic with a strong American twist, the Harvey Wallbanger, the Martini and the Manhattan are here to stay, but more recently, flamboyant tropical cocktails have proved popular. Coconut milk and exotic fruits are whizzed together to create long frothy cocktails. These concoctions are easily recreated at home now that exotic ingredients are readily available from large supermarkets.

Traditionally a cocktail is made from only two spirits or liqueurs and the bar person's worth is gauged by making them perfectly, with just enough zing, shaken or stirred to taste. As a general rule, the simpler cocktails and those that are served clear, are just stirred over ice, in a bar glass, before being strained into a serving glass. Drinks that contain fizzy liquids are never shaken, for the obvious, explosive reasons. Cocktails with large quantities of fruit juices, syrups or eggs are shaken over ice in a cocktail shaker; cocktails containing milk, cream, ice cream or coconut milk make wonderful, frothy drinks when whizzed in the blender.

"Bar speak" is something to get acquainted with: when a recipe suggests a dash of bitters that means just a shake of the bottle, while a squeeze of lemon rind does not mean the whole thing floating in the drink. The rind should be held over the glass and twisted in the fingers, so that the lemon oils drop into the cocktail: it is then discarded. "On the rocks" quite simply means served over ice and "straight up" means served just as it is, in a chilled glass.

At home you can create cocktails with no more than a cocktail shaker, large glass jug, blender and a few essential ingredients such as bitters, plain sugar syrup, and of course, a couple of bottles of your favourite spirits and liqueurs. Making cocktails is an enjoyable pastime, so stir up a drink, settle back and savour!

# Spirits, Wines and Cider

Many cocktails contain the same spirits but in different mixes or quantities, so with a small stock of different drinks a variety of cocktails is on offer. Use the best brands available for the best results.

**Brandy**

Brandy is a popular spirit distilled from grape wines. There are blended brandies available from all over the world but some of the better and more expensive brandies are French. There are two main types of French brandy: cognac and armagnac. There is also a range of fruit brandies or eaux-de-vie, such as peach, cherry and apricot, as well as calvados, which is a French fruit brandy distilled from apple wine. The American equivalent is applejack. All are perfect for use in a variety of cocktails.

**Champagne**

Use *brut* (dry) champagne or *méthode champenoise* wines when making cocktails. You'll find that they keep their sparkle a lot longer. Some of the less expensive champagne-style supermarket wines, such as the Spanish Cava, are ideal for mixing with a variety of fruit purées, freshly squeezed fruit juices and syrups.

**Cider**

A drink made from fermented apple juice. Sweet or dry cider both mix well with brandy and other spirits, as does perry, a cider made with pears. Use perry in exactly the same way as apple cider to make a tasty variation.

**Gin**

Gin is one of our favourite spirits and is ideal for mixing with many fruit juices and liqueurs, to create some of the classic cocktails. This colourless spirit is distilled from malted barley, rye or maize. Each brand uses its own very special combination of herbs, spices and citrus oils. Juniper berries give them all their most distinctive "gin" flavour.

**Ginger Wine**

A golden and green wine flavoured with citrus fruits, floral scents, herbs and ginger. It is sweet but very aromatic and spicy tasting and mixes well with spirits and red wine.

**Marsala**

This is a delicious fortified dessert wine from Sicily. It is a blend of white wine and brandy and has a sweet caramel flavour. Most people are familiar with sweet Marsala, but are unaware that a dry version with a flavour very similar to sherry can also be bought.

**Port**

A full-bodied wine, fortified with brandy during fermentation. It comes from the Douro valley of Portugal and is most commonly available as tawny, ruby, white, or Late Bottled Vintage (LBV).

**Rum**

Distilled from sugar cane and molasses and made mostly in the West Indies, particularly Jamaica, rum is available as dark or white varieties, as well as flavoured with coconut and pineapple. It is used in cocktails such as the flamboyant Blue Hawaiian, Mai Tai and Planters Punch.

**Schnapps**

Generically known as aquavit, schnapps is a popular drink in Scandinavia and Germany. It is a colourless spirit made from grain starch and is also available in assorted fruit flavours such as peach, cherry, blackcurrant, pear and apple.

**Sherry**

This fortified wine originally came from Spain but now it is also produced in a large number of other countries such as Greece, Cyprus, South Africa and Australia. It's available in a range of styles: *fino* (pale and dry), *amontillado* (medium), *manzanilla* (medium dry), *oloroso* and *amoroso* (sweetish) and *montilla* (lower in alcohol).

**Tequila**

Available in clear and golden (aged) hues, tequilas are fermented and distilled in Mexico, from the juice of the agave cactus. Tequila mixed with lime juice and a little salt is Mexico's national tipple. It is also an essential ingredient in the popular Margarita where it is mixed with Cointreau and lime.

**Vermouth**

A high-strength wine cooked with a selection of herbs, vermouth is available as extra-dry white, bitter-sweet rosé, medium-sweet bianco and sweet red. By tradition, French vermouths are drier whilst the Italian ones tend to be sweeter.

**Vodka**

A colourless spirit, distilled from rye, malt or potato starch, that originated in Eastern Europe. It has a completely neutral taste, which allows it to mix well with other spirits and fruit juices. Steeping vodka with fruits, fresh herbs and spices adds flavour and interest to the cocktail.

**Whisky**

There are various types: Scotch whisky, Irish whiskey, the American bourbon and the Canadian rye. Whisky is distilled from either malted or unmalted grains and can also be blended.

tequila

ginger wine

dark rum

champagne

white rum

sweet vermouth

calvados

Marsala

schnapps

cognac

vodka

whisky

port

gin

fino sherry

dry vermouth

# Liqueurs

Many liqueurs available today originated as medicinal tonics and a few were created by monks in their dispensaries. Liqueurs are made from a base spirit with herbs, peels of citrus fruit, spices or extracts from coffee beans.

**Amaretto**
A sweet Italian fruit-based liqueur with more than a hint of almonds and apricot, used in Hooded Claw and Cider Cup. It's made near the town of Saronno in Italy.

**Anisette**
Aniseed-flavoured liqueurs like the Italian Sambucca and the Spanish anis are often flavoured with coriander and fennel as well as aniseed. French Pernod and pastis are also anisettes, often served simply poured over plenty of ice cubes.

**Bénédictine**
Made from an old French recipe passed down by the Bénédictine monks of the abbey of Fécamp in Normandy, it is a golden-coloured brandy-based liqueur, flavoured with myrrh, other herbs and honey. It is an essential ingredient in the cocktail Sea Dog.

**Chartreuse**
A French brandy-based liqueur made from honey, herbs and spices. Originally made by Carthusian monks at La Grande Chartreuse monastery, the green liqueur has more alcohol than the yellow variety, which is flavoured with oranges and myrtle.

**Cointreau**
Sweet and syrupy, it is a colourless liqueur with a strong aromatic orange flavour and is often served poured over ice.

**Cream Liqueurs**
A mixture of cream, spirit and flavouring, such as Bailey's Irish Cream.

**Crème de Cacao**
A sweet liqueur originally made with cocoa beans from the Chouao region of Venezuela, it has a cocoa-vanilla flavour.

**Crème de Cassis**
A brandy-based blackcurrant liqueur produced in Dijon.

**Crème de Menthe**
A very sweet peppermint-flavoured liqueur, it also includes cinnamon, sage, ginger and orris and has strong digestive properties, which make it an ideal after-dinner drink.

**Curaçao**
An orange-flavoured liqueur, similar to Grand Marnier, which was originally made from the dried peel of oranges from the island of Curaçao in the West Indies. It can be blue, as used in Blue Hawaiian, white or dark orange-brown in colour.

**Drambuie**
A Scottish malt whisky-based liqueur, tinted with herbs, heather honey and spices. Often used in after-dinner coffee.

**Galliano**
A golden-coloured herb liqueur, produced in Italy, and flavoured with liquorice and aniseed.

**Grand Marnier**
A French curaçao, based on extracts from the bitter bergamot, orange and brandy. It is similar to triple sec, curaçao or Cointreau.

**Kahlúa**
A rich, brown liqueur from Mexico. Although coffee-based like Tia Maria, Kahlúa is quite different in style and is popular in the USA.

**Kümmel**
This caraway and fennel-flavoured liqueur is made mostly in Holland.

**Southern Comfort**
This American liqueur has a bourbon whiskey base and is flavoured with fruit.

**Tia Maria**
A Jamaican liqueur made from rum, Blue Mountain coffee extract and spices. It can be used for a less sweet version of Kahlúa.

## Cook's Tip
Make sure your cocktail cabinet is stocked up with a few of these essentials.

Southern Comfort    Kahlúa    Bénédictine    crème de menthe    Grand Marnier    Tia Maria    Drambuie

cherry brandy    Galliano    crème de cacao    Cointreau    blue curaçao    anisette    Amaretto    cream liqueur    green Chartreuse

# Mixers and Juices

Whether shaken or simply stirred, it is the juices
and mixers that often provide the length and body
of the cocktail. After all, where would the Bloody
Mary be without tomato juice?

These additions to the cocktail
should always be as cold as
possible. Juices are best if they
can be made from fresh fruit but,
failing that, opt for the better
quality, ready-squeezed versions
and those that are not too sweet.

**Apple Juice**
Available still or sparkling and
either clear or cloudy. Always
choose a juice with little or no
extra sugar and preservatives.

**Bitter Lemon**
A non-alcoholic fizzy mixer –
good with all white spirits. It is
made from carbonated water,
lemon, sugar and quinine.

**Coconut Milk**
Used in tropical cocktails,
coconut milk is available in cans,
as solid blocks of creamed
coconut or in a powdered form.
The blocks and powder both
require dissolving in hot water
and then should be left to cool
before use.

**Cranberry Juice**
A tangy and refreshing fruit drink
available in cartons and glass jars.
The regular cranberry juice mixes
well with spirits; other
commercially available cranberry
juices, mixed with raspberry or
blackcurrant juice, offer further
delicious flavour combinations.

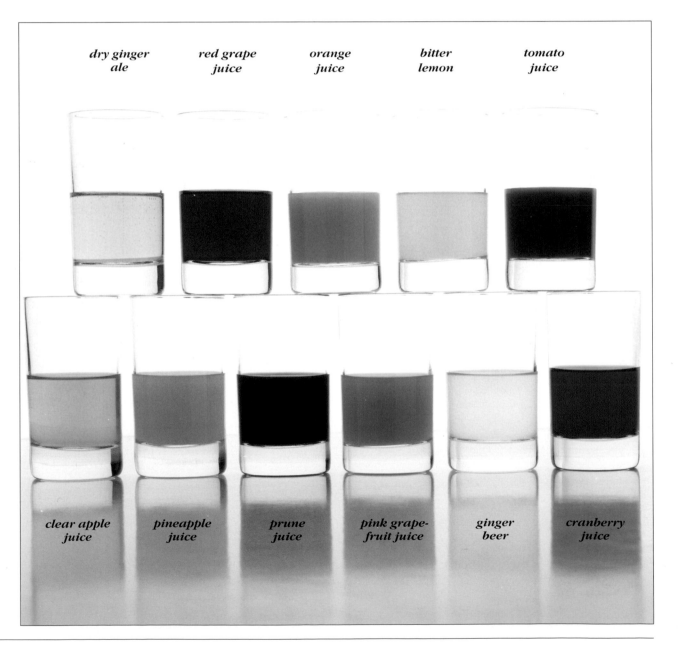

*dry ginger ale*  *red grape juice*  *orange juice*  *bitter lemon*  *tomato juice*

*clear apple juice*  *pineapple juice*  *prune juice*  *pink grape-fruit juice*  *ginger beer*  *cranberry juice*

**Ginger Ale**
Available in several varieties: dry, Canadian dry and the slightly sweeter American dry. A non-alcoholic mixer, it is made from carbonated water, ginger extract and sugar. Mixes well with whisky, bourbon and gin and is used in Kew Pimms.

**Ginger Beer**
A fermented drink made from ginger, sugar, water and yeast. The alcohol content in ginger beer is negligible.

**Lemonade**
Usually a non-alcoholic fizzy soft drink. Alcoholic and some traditional lemonade varieties are now available.

**Orange Juice**
For best results, either squeeze fresh oranges yourself or purchase chilled orange juice made from 100% fresh fruit. These have nothing added and certainly no extra sugar. Other orange juices are mostly made with sweetened concentrates.

**Passion-fruit Cordial and Nectar**
These are made with concentrated passion-fruit juice and natural flavourings. The cordial is very strong and needs diluting, to taste.

**Pineapple Juice**
The sweet and sour flavour of pineapple juice is imperative in many tropical cocktails. Use either freshly-squeezed or cartons, but preferably use the less sweet varieties.

**Pink Grapefruit Juice**
Often made from Florida pink grapefruit which are naturally sweet, it mixes well with white spirits. Look out for juices made from freshly squeezed fruit.

**Prune Juice**
This is imported from America and is made from a concentrate of dried prunes with no added sugar or preservatives.

**Red Grape Juice**
A light and fruity juice which is useful for making non-alcoholic cocktails. Choose cartons to keep in the cupboard and once opened, store in the fridge for up to three days.

**Soda Water**
A mixer containing sparkling water and bicarbonate of soda. Traditionally mixed with whisky and good to use when making long thirst-quenching cocktails. Sparkling mineral water can be used in its place.

**Tomato Juice**
An excellent versatile mixer available in thick or thin consistencies. It can be found, mixed with clam juice, in a Canadian product called Clamato.

**Tonic Water**
A good old-fashioned mixer which is used with gin, vodka or whisky. Available in a low calorie variety. It contains a small amount of quinine.

# Added Flavours

These are the little extras that make all the difference between a good or a boring cocktail.

**Bitters, Syrups and Sauces**
The most widely used is angostura bitters, made in the West Indies from cloves, cinnamon, gentian, mace, nutmeg, quinine, prunes and other barks, stems and herbs. It has a distinctive flavour and rosy-red hue when a few drops are used. Grenadine and lime cordial both add sweetness and hints of their own individual flavours of pomegranate and lime. Grenadine is also used for its pink/red colour which creates a glowing band at the bottom of a Mai-Tai and a Tequila Sunrise.
  Other herbs and spices are vital for their flavours and are used in making Tabasco sauce and Worcestershire sauce, both of which are used for maximum impact in a Bloody Mary. Balsamic and cider vinegars add a tart flavour but are less sour than lemon or lime juice.

**Herbs**
Ground celery seeds, fresh mint or lemon balm leaves and, during the summer months, fresh borage, chive or thyme flowers add hints of aromatic flavours. These are used to great effect for their individual tastes and also for added colour and decoration.

**Spices**
Freshly-grated nutmeg, cloves, bruised cardamom pods, sticks of cinnamon and a pinch of cayenne, all pep up a basic punch or egg-nog; and freshly-grated or creamed horseradish and fresh ginger add a zing all of their own to the simplest of juices. Use any spice with care, since an over-eager hand can easily upset the delicate balance of a cocktail. Taste as you go along and then add a little more if liked.

# Cocktail Equipment

To make a successful cocktail you need a few essential pieces of barman's equipment. The most vital and flamboyant is the cocktail shaker; what you have in the cupboard can usually be substituted for the rest. The equipment is listed below in descending order of importance.

**Cocktail Shaker**
A cocktail shaker is used for those cocktails made with juices and syrups that need good mixing but do not depend upon being crystal clear. Shakers are made of stainless steel, silver, perspex or tough glass. The Boston shaker is made of two cup-type containers that fit over each other, one normally made of glass, the other of metal. This type is often preferred by professional bar staff. For beginners the classic three-piece shaker is easier to handle, with its base to hold the ice and liquids, a top fitted with a built-in strainer and a tight-fitting cap.

**Blender**
Goblet blenders are the best shape for mixing cocktails that need to be aerated, to create a frothy cocktail, or to be blended with finely crushed ice. A word of warning: do not be tempted to crush the ice in the blender, since this will blunt the blade. Opt for a tea towel or cloth bag and a rolling pin and save your blender from ruin.

**Ice Bag or Cloth**
Essential for holding ice cubes when crushing, either to roughly cracked lumps or to fine snow. Both the ice bag and cloth must be scrupulously clean.

**Wooden Hammer**
For crushing the ice, the end of a wooden rolling pin will also work well.

**Tot Measures or Measuring Jug**
For measuring out the required quantities. The measurements can be in single (22.5 ml) or double (45 ml) bar measures, fluid ounces or millilitres. Do not switch from one type of measurement to another. 1 measure equals 22.5 ml/ $1^1/_2$ tbsp.

**Strainer**
Used when pouring drinks from shaker or bar glass to cocktail glass, the best strainers are made from stainless steel and look like a flat spoon, with holes and with a curl of wire on the underside. These are held over the top of the glass to hold the fruit and ice back.

**Mixing Jug or Bar Glass**
It is useful to have a container in which to mix and stir drinks that are not shaken. The glass or jug should be large enough to hold two or three drinks. This method is intended for drinks that are meant to be clear, not cloudy.

**Corkscrew**
For the obvious reasons. The fold away type, with a can opener and bottle-top opener, is very useful to have to hand for all drink-opening possibilities.

**Bar Spoon**
These long-handled spoons can reach to the bottom of the tallest tumblers and are used for mixing the drink directly in the glass. Some have a disc base at the top.

**Muddler**
A long stick with a bulbous end, which is used for crushing sugar or mint leaves, and so is particularly useful when creating juleps. There are a variety of sizes. They are either used like a pestle in a bar glass, or, in a smaller version, in the individual glass.

**Lemon Knife and Squeezer**
Citrus fruit are vital in many cocktails; a good quality sharp knife is required for cutting fruit and the squeezer for extracting juice. Fruit juice presses are quicker to use but more costly.

**Nutmeg Grater**
A tiny grater with small holes, for grating this hard nut over egg-nogs and frothy drinks.

**Straws, Swizzle and Cocktail Sticks**
Used for the finishing decorative touches that complete a cocktail.

**Zester and Canelle Knife**
For presenting fruit when dressing glasses. If you do not already have these, do not run out and buy them, since drinks can look equally attractive with more simply sliced fruit.

Right: *1: blender; 2: cocktail shakers; 3: fruit juice press; 4: wooden hammer; 5: canelle knife; 6: corkscrew; 7: bar spoon; 8: strainer; 9: drinking straws; 10: tot measures; 11: measuring spoons; 12: cup measures; 13: cocktail sticks; 14: swizzle sticks; 15: nutmeg grater; 16: cloth; 17: sharp knife.*

# Glasses

Glasses should always be washed and dried with a glass cloth to ensure they are sparkling clean. Although some recipes suggest chilled glasses, don't be tempted to put the best crystal in the freezer; leave it at the back of the fridge instead.

**Cocktail or Martini Glasses**
Classic and elegant, this glass is a wide conical bowl on a tall stem, which keeps warm hands away from the drink. It holds about 150 ml/$^1$/$_4$ pint.

**Collins Glass**
The tallest of the tumblers, narrow with perfectly straight sides, it holds about 300 ml/$^1$/$_2$ pint and is typically used for long drinks made with fresh juices or topped up with soda.

**Old-fashioned Glass**
Classic shorts (whisky) tumblers are used for shorter drinks, which are served "on the rocks". They hold about 175 ml/6 fl oz.

**Highball Glass**
The middle-sized tumbler and the most used. It holds about 250 ml/8 fl oz.

**Liqueur Glass**
A tiny glass for small measures of about 50 ml/2 fl oz.

**Brandy Balloon or Snifter**
This glass has been designed to trap the fragrance of the brandy in the bowl of the glass. The cocktail is further helped by being cupped in the palms of the hands to warm it gently and release the aromas.

**Large Cocktail Goblets**
These vary in size and shape and are used for serving larger frothy drinks, such as tropical cocktails and Piña Coladas. The wider rims of these glasses leave plenty of room for flamboyant decoration.

**Champagne Glasses**
Champagne can be poured either into attractive and old-fashioned champagne bowls or tall and slim flutes. The champagne flute is the more acceptable glass to use as it is more efficient at conserving the fizz and the bubbles.

**Red Wine Balloon**
The most useful size of wine glass, holding 300 ml/$^1$/$_2$ pint. They are only filled to half their capacity to allow the wine to be swirled around inside.

**White Wine Glass**
This is a long-stemmed medium-sized glass that, once again, keeps warm hands away from the chilled wine or cocktail.

**Pousse-café**
A thin and narrow glass standing on a short stem. Used for floating or layered stronger liqueur cocktails.

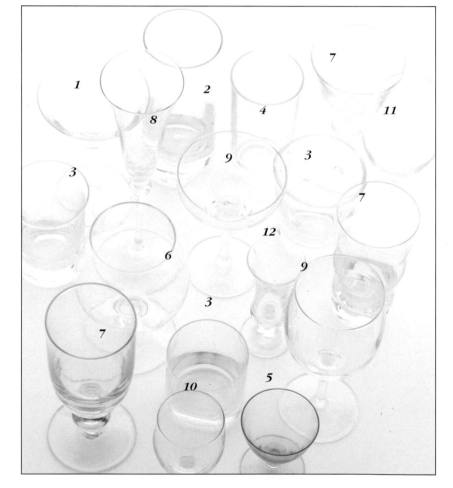

Above: *1: cocktail glass; 2: Collins glass; 3: old-fashioned glass; 4: highball glass; 5: liqueur glass; 6: brandy balloon; 7: large cocktail goblet; 8: champagne flute; 9: champagne bowl; 10: red wine balloon; 11: white wine glass; 12: pousse-café.*

# Garnishes

It is far more eye-catching not to over-dress cocktails, otherwise they all too quickly look like a fruit salad. Less is best! These little extra edible garnishes should reflect the contents of the glass.

Frosting glasses with salt and sugar is a simple but effective touch, which hardly needs much extra help or assistance.

Edible garnishes are always best and should reflect the contents of the cocktail. Citrus fruit are widely used because they stay appetizing to look at and can be cut in advance and kept covered in the fridge, for a day, until required. Apple, pear and banana are suitable, but they do discolour on exposure to the air; dip them in lemon juice first.

Soft fruit such as strawberries, fresh cherries, peaches, apricots and redcurrants make fabulous splashes of colour and add a delicious flavour, but are only available during the summer.

The maraschino cherry is a popular option and the never ending supply of exotic fruits available all year round, such as mango, pineapple and star fruit together offer endless decorative possibilities.

But not all garnishes and decorations are fruit-based. Grated chocolate and nutmeg adorn egg-nogs and flips, while some Martinis call for a green olive – always opt for those in brine and not in oil. Plain or steeped-chilli vodka can stand pickled chillies and the Gibson (a dry Martini cocktail) couldn't be a Gibson without a white pearl onion to complete it.

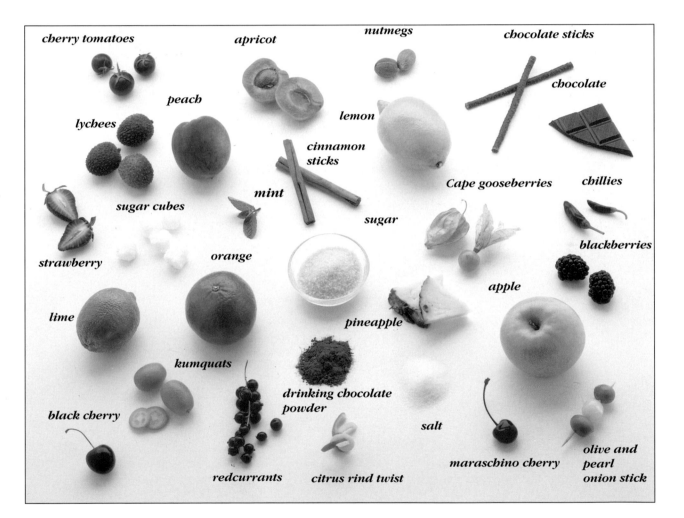

cherry tomatoes · apricot · nutmegs · chocolate sticks · chocolate · peach · lemon · lychees · cinnamon sticks · Cape gooseberries · chillies · mint · sugar · blackberries · strawberry · sugar cubes · orange · apple · lime · pineapple · kumquats · drinking chocolate powder · salt · black cherry · redcurrants · citrus rind twist · maraschino cherry · olive and pearl onion stick

# Crushing Ice

Some cocktails require cracked or crushed ice for adding to glasses, or a finely crushed ice snow for blending. It is not a good idea to do this in a blender or food processor as you may find it makes the blade blunt.

# Making Decorative Ice Cubes

Decorative ice cubes can instantly jazz up simple cocktails. Flavour and colour ice cubes with fruit juices or bitters and freeze as normal.

**1** Lay a cloth on a work surface and cover half of the cloth with ice cubes. Alternatively, place the ice cubes in a cloth ice bag.

**2** Fold the cloth over and, using the end of a rolling pin or a wooden mallet, strike the ice firmly, several times, until you achieve the required fineness.

**1** Fill each compartment of an ice cube tray half-full with water and place in the freezer for 2–3 hours or until the water has frozen.

**2** Prepare the fruit, olives, mint leaves, lemon rind, raisins or borage flowers and dip each briefly in water. Place in the ice-cube trays and freeze again.

**3** Spoon or scrape the fine ice snow into glasses or a jug. Fine ice snow must be used immediately, but cracked or roughly crushed ice can be stored in the freezer in plastic bags.

**3** Top up the ice cube trays with water and return to the freezer to freeze completely. Use as required.

# Frosting Glasses

Frosting adds both to the look and the taste of a cocktail. Use celery salt, grated coconut, grated chocolate, coloured sugars or cocoa for a similar effect. Once frosted, place the glass in the fridge to chill, until needed.

# Shaking Cocktails

Cocktails that contain sugar syrups or creams require more than just a stir and are combined and chilled by briefly shaking together with ice. Remember that it is only possible to shake one or two servings at a time.

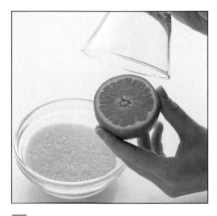

**1** Hold the glass upside-down, so the juice does not run down the glass. Rub the rim of the glass with the cut surface of a lemon, lime, orange or even a slice of fresh pineapple.

**2** Keeping the glass upside-down, dip the rim into a shallow layer of sugar or salt. Re-dip the glass, if necessary, so the rim is well-coated.

**1** Fill the cocktail shaker two-thirds full with ice cubes and pour in the spirits; add the mixers, if not sparkling, and the flavouring ingredients.

**2** Put the lid on the shaker. Hold the shaker firmly, keeping the lid in place with one hand.

**3** Stand the glass upright and leave it until the salt and sugar has dried on the rim, then chill.

**3** Shake vigorously, for about 10 seconds to blend simple concoctions and for 20–30 seconds for drinks with sugar syrups or eggs. By this time the outside of the shaker should feel chilled.

**4** Remove the small lid and pour into the prepared glass, using a strainer if the shaker is not already fitted with one.

# Making Basic Sugar Syrup

A sugar syrup is sometimes preferable to crystal sugars for sweetening cocktails, since it immediately blends with the other ingredients.

*Makes about 750 ml/24 fl oz*

INGREDIENTS
350 g/12 oz caster sugar
600 ml/20 fl oz water

**1** Place the sugar in a heavy-based pan with the water, and heat gently over a low heat. Stir with a wooden spoon until the sugar has dissolved.

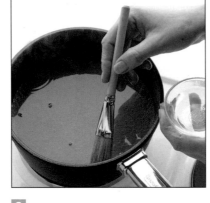

**2** Brush the sides of the pan with a pastry brush dampened in water to remove any sugar crystals that might cause the sugar syrup to crystallize.

**3** Bring to the boil for 3–5 minutes. Skim off any scum and, when no more appears, remove the pan from the heat.

**4** Cool and pour into clean, dry, airtight bottles. Keep in the fridge for up to one month.

# Making Flavoured Syrups

Syrup can be flavoured with any ingredient you like. Add to the basic syrup, bring to the boil, then bottle with the syrup.

*Makes about 450 ml/15 fl oz*

INGREDIENTS
900 g/2 lb very ripe soft or stone fruit, washed
350 g/12 oz caster sugar

### COOK'S TIP
Raspberries, black or redcurrants, plums and peaches all make delicious flavoured syrups.

**1** Place the washed fruit of your choice in a bowl and, using the bottom of a rolling pin, a wooden pestle or a potato masher, crush the fruit to release the juices. Cover and leave overnight to concentrate the flavour.

**2** Strain the purée through a cloth bag or piece of muslin. Gather the corners of the cloth together and twist them tightly to remove as much juice as possible. Measure the amount of juice and add 225 g/8 oz sugar to every 300 ml/½ pint fruit juice.

**3** Place the pan over a low heat and gently stir until all the sugar has dissolved. Continue as in the recipe for basic sugar syrup. The syrup will keep in the fridge for up to one month.

# Making Flavoured Spirits

Gin, vodka and white rum can be left to steep and absorb the flavours of a wide variety of soft fruits.

## *Makes 1.2 litre/40 fl oz*

INGREDIENTS
450 g/1 lb raspberries,
  strawberries, pineapple or sloes
225 g/8 oz caster sugar
1 litre/35 fl oz gin or vodka

### VARIATIONS
Vodka and sliced bananas;
white rum and fresh pineapple;
gin and drained, canned lychees;
sliced peaches or apricots; brandy
and plums or apricots.

# Steeping Spirits

Steeping any spirit with a strong flavouring ingredient, such as chillies, creates an interestingly flavoured spirit.

## *Makes 1 litre/35 fl oz*

INGREDIENTS
1 litre/35 fl oz sherry or vodka
25–50 g/1–2 oz small red chillies,
  or to taste

**1** Place the fruit in a wide-necked jar and add the sugar. If using sloes, prick them with a needle or fine skewer, to release their flavour.

**2** Add the spirit. Cover tightly. Leave in a cool, dark place for a month, shaking gently every week.

**1** Wash and dry the chillies, discarding any chillies that are less than perfect. Using a cocktail stick, prick the chillies all over to release their flavours.

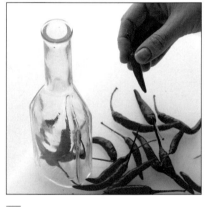

**2** Pack the chillies tightly into a sterilized bottle.

**3** Strain through muslin or a cloth bag and squeeze out the rest of the liquid from the steeped fruit.

**4** Return the flavoured spirit to a clean bottle, seal and store it in a cool, dark place.

**3** Top up with sherry or vodka. Fit the cork tightly and leave in a dark place for at least ten days or up to two months.

### VARIATIONS
Try the following interesting alternatives: gin with cumin seeds, star anise or juniper berries; brandy with 25 g/1 oz peeled and sliced fresh root ginger or 15 g/$^{1}/_{2}$ oz whole cloves; vodka with 50 g/2 oz washed raisins or 1–2 tbsp cracked black peppercorns; rum with 2–3 pricked vanilla pods. The amount of flavouring used is a question of personal taste.

# Gin Smash

This simple and very refreshing cocktail can be made with fresh peppermint, apple mint or black mint to produce three uniquely flavoured drinks. Use the variety of mint you prefer.

VARIATION
Use Southern Comfort or bourbon in place of the gin.

## Serves 1

INGREDIENTS
15 ml/1 tbsp caster sugar
4 fresh sprigs of mint
2 measures/45 ml/3 tbsp dry gin

*gin*

*caster sugar*

*mint*

**1** Dissolve the sugar in a little water in the cocktail shaker.

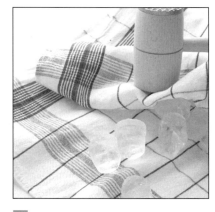

**2** Place some ice cubes in a clean tea towel and crush them finely.

**3** Add the mint to the cocktail shaker and, using a muddler, bruise and press the juices out of the mint.

**4** Half-fill the shaker with the cracked ice and add the gin.

**5** Put on the top and shake the cocktail for about 20 seconds, to mix the gin with the mint.

**6** Strain the cocktail into a small wine glass filled with crushed ice. If liked, add fresh mint sprigs and drinking straws.

# Gall Bracer

Short and smart, this drink is served on the rocks, in a tumbler for a man or in a delicate long-stemmed cocktail glass, with a maraschino cherry, for a lady.

## *Serves 1*

INGREDIENTS
2 dashes angostura bitters
2 dashes grenadine
2 measures/45 ml/3 tbsp whisky
lemon rind
maraschino cherry, to decorate
   (optional)

*grenadine*

*maraschino cherry*

*whisky*

*angostura bitters*

**1** Half-fill a bar glass with ice. Add the angostura bitters, grenadine and whisky and stir well to chill.

**2** Place some ice in a short tumbler and pour the cocktail over it.

**3** Holding the lemon rind between the fingers, squeeze out the oils and juices into the cocktail. Discard the lemon rind.

**4** Add a cherry, if you like.

## VARIATION

For a longer drink, top up with soda or sparkling mineral water, or for a cocktail called a Gall Trembler substitute gin for the whisky and add more bitters.

# Gibson

Well loved in Japan, this is a version of the Martini with a small white onion in it, rather than the twist of lemon. You may prefer a higher proportion of gin.

### *Serves 1*

INGREDIENTS
½ measure/10 ml/2 tsp extra-dry
vermouth
1 scant measure/20 ml/1¼ tbsp
extra-dry gin
2 pearl onions, to decorate

*extra-dry vermouth*

*gin*

*pearl onions*

## VARIATION
Add a touch more dry vermouth and a twist of lemon and you have an Australian Kangaroo.

**1** Pour the vermouth into a bar glass of ice, stir briskly and then pour out. Only the vermouth that clings to the ice and glass should be used.

**2** Add the gin and stir for at least 30 seconds, to chill well.

**3** Strain into a martini glass either on the rocks or straight up.

**4** Thread the pearl onions on to a cocktail stick and add to the drink.

# Brandy Alexander

A warming digestif, made from a blend of crème de cacao, brandy and double cream, that can be served at the end of the meal with coffee.

## Serves 1

INGREDIENTS
1 measure/22.5 ml/1$^1$/$_2$ tbsp
    brandy
1 measure/22.5 ml/1$^1$/$_2$ tbsp
    crème de cacao
1 measure/22.5 ml/1$^1$/$_2$ tbsp
    double cream
whole nutmeg, grated,
    to decorate

 crème de cacao

 nutmeg

double cream

 brandy

**I** Half-fill the cocktail shaker with ice and pour in the brandy, crème de cacao and, finally, the cream.

**2** Shake for about 20 seconds, to mix together well.

## VARIATION

Warm the brandy and the double cream gently and add to a blender with the crème de cacao. Whizz until frothy. Serve with a cinnamon stick.

**3** Strain the chilled cocktail into a small wine glass.

**4** Finely grate a little nutmeg over the top of the cocktail.

# Perfect Manhattan

When making Manhattans it's a matter of preference whether you use sweet vermouth, dry vermouth or a mixture. Both of the former require a dash of angostura bitters.

### *Serves 1*

INGREDIENTS
2 measures/45 ml/3 tbsp rye
  whisky
¹/₄ measure/5 ml/1 tsp dry
  French vermouth
¹/₄ measure/5 ml/1 tsp sweet
  Italian vermouth
lemon rind and a maraschino
  cherry, to decorate

*sweet vermouth*

*maraschino cherry*

*whisky*

*dry vermouth*

*lemon rind*

## VARIATION

Create a Skyscraper by adding a dash of angostura bitters, a teaspoon of maraschino cherry juice, and top up with ginger ale.

**1** Pour the whisky and vermouths into a bar glass of ice. Stir well for about 30 seconds, to mix and chill.

**2** Strain, on the rocks or straight up, into a chilled cocktail glass.

**3** Using a canelle knife, pare away a small strip of lemon rind. Tie it into a knot, to help release the oils from the rind, and drop it into the cocktail.

**4** To finish, add a maraschino cherry with its stalk left intact.

# Margarita

Traditionally this popular strong apéritif is
made with tequila and Cointreau, but it is also good
made with vodka and triple sec (a term
used for white curaçao).

## VARIATION

Replace the Cointreau with blue
curaçao for an interesting colour
and flavour.

## Serves 1

INGREDIENTS
1 measure/22.5 ml/1½ tbsp
   tequila
1 measure/22.5 ml/1½ tbsp
   Cointreau
⅔ measure/15 ml/1 tbsp lime
   juice
wedge of fresh lime, fine salt
   crystals, and cucumber peel,
   to decorate

*tequila*

*salt*

*Cointreau*

*lime juice*

*cucumber peel*

**1** Rub the rim of the glass with a
wedge of fresh lime.

**2** Invert the glass into fine salt, to
create a rim of salt. Turn the glass the
right way up and chill until required.

**3** Pour the tequila and Cointreau,
with the lime juice, into a cocktail shaker
filled with ice. Shake for 20 seconds.

**4** Carefully strain the cocktail into the
frosted glass.

**5** Using a sharp knife or vegetable
peeler, cut a long thin strip of green peel
from a whole cucumber.

**6** Trim the cucumber peel to size and
thread it on to a cocktail stick. Add to
the glass to decorate.

# Hooded Claw

Syrupy-sweet prune juice with Amaretto and Cointreau makes a delicious digestif when poured over finely crushed ice snow.

### *Serves 4*

INGREDIENTS
5 measures/120 ml/4 fl oz prune
    juice
2 measures/45 ml/3 tbsp
    Amaretto
1 measure/22.5 ml/1¹/₂ tbsp
    Cointreau

*Amaretto*

*Cointreau*

*prune juice*

## VARIATION
Mix 6 parts prune juice with 1 part elderflower cordial, for a tangy, non-alcoholic version. Serve it on the rocks and super-cold.

**1** Pour the prune juice, Amaretto and Cointreau together into a cocktail shaker half-filled with ice.

**2** Shake the cocktail for 20 seconds, to chill well.

**3** Loosely fill four small liqueur glasses with finely crushed ice snow.

**4** Strain the drink into the glasses and serve with short drinking straws.

# Bitter Gimlet

An old-fashioned apéritif, which could easily be turned into a longer drink by topping up with chilled tonic or soda water.

## Serves 1

INGREDIENTS
1 lime, cut into wedges
1 measure/22.5 ml/1½ tbsp gin
2 dashes angostura bitters
slice and rind of lime, to decorate

*lime wedges*

*lime decoration*

*angostura bitters*

*gin*

## VARIATION

Add a teaspoon of sugar, for a sweeter version, or add a dash or two of crème de menthe to create a Fallen Angel.

**1** Place the lime at the bottom of the bar glass and, using a muddler, press the juice out of the lime.

**2** Add cracked ice, the gin and the bitters and stir well, until cold.

**3** Strain the cocktail into a short tumbler over ice cubes.

**4** Add a triangle of lime rind to the drink and use a slice of lime to decorate the rim of the glass.

# Chilli Vodkatini

Not quite a Martini, but almost. Over the years the proportions of spirit to vermouth have varied widely, with the vodka becoming almost overwhelming. Be sure to have your chilli vodka made well in advance and ready to use.

### VARIATION

For the classic Martini, use gin, but serve with a twist of lemon. Mix plain vodka and dry vermouth for a Vodka Martini. Add an olive and it becomes a Vodka Gibson.

## Serves 1

INGREDIENTS
1 measure/22.5 ml/1¹/₂ tbsp chilli vodka
¹/₄ measure/5 ml/1 tsp medium or dry French vermouth
2 small pickled or vodka-soaked chillies, to decorate
1 pitted green olive, to decorate

*chilli vodka*

*dry vermouth*

*chilli-stuffed olive*

**1** Add the chilli vodka to a bar glass of ice and mix for about 30 seconds, until the outside of the glass has frosted.

**2** Add the vermouth to a chilled cocktail glass and swirl it round the inside of the glass, to moisten it. Discard any remaining vermouth.

**3** Cut one of the pickled chillies in half and discard the seeds. Stuff the pitted green olive with the chilli.

**4** Thread the stuffed olive on to a cocktail stick, together with the remaining chilli.

**5** Strain the cocktail into the prepared cocktail glass.

**6** Add the olive and chilli decoration to the drink before serving.

# Gin Crusta

Prepare the glass in advance and keep it chilled in the fridge ready for instant use! The depth of pink colour will depend on the strength of the maraschino cherry juice.

## VARIATION

Make in the same way with whisky, Southern Comfort, brandy or rum.

### Serves 1

INGREDIENTS
1 lemon
30 ml/2 tbsp golden granulated
    sugar
3 dashes sugar syrup
2 dashes maraschino cherry juice
2 dashes angostura bitters
1 measure/22.5 ml/1½ tbsp dry
    gin

 *angostura bitters*

 *maraschino cherry juice*

*golden granulated sugar*

*lemon juice*

*gin*

*sugar syrup*

 *lemon rind*

**1** Cut both ends off the lemon and, using a sharp knife or canelle knife, peel the lemon thinly, as you would an apple, in one long continuous piece.

**2** Halve the whole lemon and rub the edge of a glass with one half.

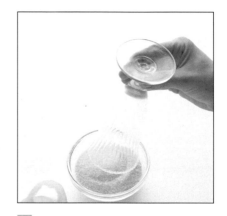

**3** Turn the glass upside-down and dip it into the granulated sugar, to create a decorative rim.

**4** Arrange the lemon rind in a scroll on the inside of the glass.

**5** Place the sugar syrup, maraschino cherry juice, angostura bitters, gin and juice of ¼ of the lemon in a cocktail shaker, half-filled with ice.

**6** Shake for about 30 seconds and carefully strain into the prepared glass.

# Airstrike

A variation on a Val d'Isère Shooter, similar in idea to the Italian Flaming Sambucca.

*Serves 1*

INGREDIENTS
2 measures/45 ml/3 tbsp Galliano
1 measure/22.5 ml/1$^1$/$_2$ tbsp
    brandy
1 star anise

 *Galliano*

 *star anise*

*brandy*

## VARIATION
Use all Sambucca and float two or three coffee beans on the surface instead of the star anise before lighting.

**1** Put the Galliano and brandy in a small saucepan and heat very gently, until just warm.

**2** Carefully pour into a heat-resistant glass standing on a small plate or saucer; add the star anise.

**3** Using a lighted taper or long match, pass the flame over the surface of the drink to ignite it. The flame will be low and very pale, so be careful not to burn yourself.

**4** Leave to burn for a couple of minutes, until the star anise has sizzled a little and released extra aroma into the drink. Leave to cool slightly before drinking. The top of the glass will be hot!

# B52

This cocktail depends on the difference in specific weight or densities of each of the liqueurs to remain strictly separated in layers.

## Serves 1

INGREDIENTS
1 measure/22.5 ml/1¹/₂ tbsp
   Kahlúa
1 measure/22.5 ml/1¹/₂ tbsp
   Grand Marnier
1 measure/22.5 ml/1¹/₂ tbsp
   Bailey's Irish Cream

Grand Marnier

Bailey's Irish Cream

Kahlúa

## VARIATION

Create a similar layered effect with equal quantities of Bailey's, Kahlúa and vodka, layered in that order. Or try Chartreuse, cherry brandy and kümmel, with cumin seeds floated on the top.

**1** In a small shooter or pousse-café glass, pour a 2 cm/³/4 in layer of Kahlúa.

**2** Hold a cold teaspoon upside-down, only just touching the surface of the Kahlúa and the side of the glass.

**3** Slowly and carefully pour the Grand Marnier over the back of the teaspoon, to create a second layer.

**4** In the same way, carefully pour the Bailey's over the back of a second clean teaspoon, to create a final layer. This layer in fact will form the middle layer and push the Grand Marnier to the top!

# Coffee and Chocolate Flip

Since the egg is not cooked, use only the freshest eggs. Drambuie can be used instead of brandy for a hint of honey, but don't add the sugar. Substitute Tia Maria for the Kahlúa, for a less sweet version.

## VARIATION
Shake together equal quantities of Kahlúa, chocolate-flavoured milk and coffee. Serve on the rocks.

### Serves 1

INGREDIENTS
1 egg
1 tsp caster sugar
1 measure/22.5 ml/1¹/₂ tbsp brandy
1 measure/22.5 ml/1¹/₂ tbsp Kahlúa
5 ml/1 tsp instant coffee granules
3 measures/70 ml/4¹/₂ tbsp double
    cream
drinking chocolate powder or grated
    chocolate, to decorate

*instant coffee granules*

*egg*

*caster sugar*

*drinking chocolate powder*

*double cream*        *Kahlúa*

*brandy*

**1** Separate the egg and lightly beat the egg white until frothy and white.

**2** In a separate bowl or glass, beat the egg yolk with the sugar.

**3** In a small saucepan, gently warm together the brandy, Kahlúa, coffee granules and cream.

**4** Whisk the cooled cream mixture into the egg yolk.

**5** Add the egg white to the egg and cream and pour the mixture briefly back and forth between two glasses, until the mixture is smooth.

**6** Pour into a tall glass over coarsely crushed ice and sprinkle the top with drinking chocolate powder.

# Cranberry Kiss

A delicious full-flavoured cocktail, with the tang of cranberry and pink grapefruit juices and the sweetness of Marsala.

## Serves 1

INGREDIENTS

2 measures/45 ml/3 tbsp cranberry
   juice
1 measure/22.5 ml/1$^1$/$_2$ tbsp
   brandy
2 measures/45 ml/3 tbsp pink
   grapefruit juice
2 measures/45 ml/3 tbsp Marsala
redcurrant string, to decorate
1 egg white, lightly beaten, to
   decorate
15 g/$^1$/$_2$ oz caster sugar, to
   decorate

*caster sugar*

*egg white*

*brandy*

*cranberry juice*

*pink grapefruit juice*

*Marsala*

*redcurrant string*

### VARIATION

Shake together cranberry and pineapple juice with coconut milk. Add vodka or gin to taste.

**1** Lightly brush the redcurrants with the egg white.

**2** Shake caster sugar over the redcurrants, to cover them in a light frosting. Leave aside to dry.

**3** Place the cranberry juice with the brandy and grapefruit juice in a cocktail shaker full of crushed ice and shake for 20 seconds to mix.

**4** Strain into a well-chilled glass.

**5** Tilt the glass slightly, before slowly pouring the Marsala into the drink down the side of the glass.

**6** Serve decorated with the frosted redcurrant string.

# Grasshopper

A minted, creamy cocktail in an attractive shade of green. If you use dark crème de cacao the cocktail will not be as vibrant a green colour but you'll find that it will taste just as good.

## Serves 1

INGREDIENTS
2 measures/45 ml/3 tbsp crème de menthe
2 measures/45 ml/3 tbsp light crème de cacao
2 measures/45 ml/3 tbsp double cream
melted plain chocolate, to decorate

*double cream*

*crème de menthe*

*crème de cacao*

*plain chocolate*

## VARIATION

Process in a blender, with crushed ice, for a smoother consistency. For a Scandinavian Freeze, mix vodka with crème de cacao and a scoop of vanilla ice cream and process just until smooth.

**1** Measure the crème de menthe and crème de cacao into a cocktail shaker and add the cream.

**2** Add some cracked ice and shake well for 20 seconds.

**3** Strain the cocktail into a tumbler of finely-cracked ice.

**4** To decorate, spread the melted chocolate evenly over a plastic board and leave to cool and harden. Using a sharp knife draw the blade across the chocolate to create curls. Add to the top of the cocktail and serve.

# Tequila Sunset

A variation on the popular party drink which can be mixed and chilled in a jug, ready to pour into glasses, and finished off at the last minute with the addition of crème de cassis and honey.

## Serves 1

INGREDIENTS

1 measure/22.5 ml/1$^{1}$/$_{2}$ tbsp clear or golden tequila

5 measures/120 ml/ 4 fl oz lemon juice, chilled

1 measure/22.5 ml/1$^{1}$/$_{2}$ tbsp orange juice, chilled

10–30 ml/1–2 tbsp clear honey

$^{2}$/$_{3}$ measure/15 ml/1 tbsp crème de cassis

crème de cassis

lemon juice

tequila

clear honey

orange juice

**1** Pour the tequila and then the lemon and orange juices straight into a well-chilled cocktail glass.

**2** Using a swizzle stick, mix the ingredients by twisting the stick between the palms of your hands.

**3** Drizzle the honey into the centre of the cocktail and it will fall and create a layer at the bottom of the glass.

**4** Add the crème de cassis, but do not stir. It will create a glowing layer above the honey at the bottom of the glass.

## VARIATION

To make a Tequila Sunrise, mix 2 parts tequila with 6 parts orange juice and 2 parts grenadine and stir gently together.

# Vunderful

A long, lazy Sunday afternoon tipple, conjured up in the heat of Zimbabwe. Leave the fruits in the gin for as long as possible.

## *Serves 20*

INGREDIENTS
400 g/14 oz can lychees
2 peaches, sliced
600 ml/20 fl oz gin

For each person you will need:
1 measure/22.5 ml/1½ tbsp Pimms
2–3 dashes angostura bitters
5 measures/120 ml/4 fl oz chilled
   tonic water or lemonade
slices of lime, to decorate

*angostura bitters*

*Pimms*

*slice of lime*

*peaches*

*gin*

*lychees*

*lemonade*

**1**  Strain the lychees from the syrup and place them in a wide-necked jar with the peach slices and the gin. Leave overnight or for up to a month.

**2**  Mix for each person, in a large bar glass or jug, 1 measure/22.5ml/1½ tbsp lychee gin with 1 measure/22.5 ml/1½ tbsp Pimms and add bitters to taste.

**3**  Strain into tall tumblers filled with ice cubes.

**4**  Add chilled tonic water or lemonade, to taste.

**5**  Put some of the drained gin-soaked lychees and peaches into each glass and add a muddler, with which to stir and crush the fruit into the drink.

**6**  Add a half slice of lime to the rim of the glass and serve.

# Blue Hawaiian

This drink can be decorated as flamboyantly as Carmen Miranda's head-dress with a mixture of fruits and leaves. An eye-catching colour, but you'll find it very drinkable.

## Serves 1

INGREDIENTS
1 measure/22.5 ml/1½ tbsp blue
   curaçao
1 measure/22.5 ml/1½ tbsp
   coconut cream
2 measures/45 ml/3 tbsp white
   rum
2 measures/45 ml/3 tbsp pineapple
   juice

TO DECORATE:
leaves and wedge of pineapple
slice of prickly pear
wedge of lime
maraschino cherry

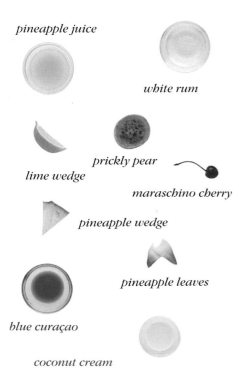

*pineapple juice*

*white rum*

*prickly pear*

*lime wedge*

*maraschino cherry*

*pineapple wedge*

*pineapple leaves*

*blue curaçao*

*coconut cream*

## VARIATION

Pour equal quantities of vodka and blue curaçao over ice. Top up with lemonade for a Blue Lagoon or add equal quantities of gin and curaçao, plus angostura bitters, for a Blue Cloak.

**1** Put the curacao, coconut cream and white rum in a blender. Process very briefly until the colour is even.

**2** Place ice cubes between a tea towel and crush to a fine snow with a wooden hammer or rolling pin.

**3** Add the pineapple juice to the blender and process the mixture once more, until frothy.

**4** Spoon the crushed ice into a large cocktail glass or goblet.

**5** Pour the cocktail from the blender over the crushed ice.

**6** Decorate with the pineapple leaves and wedge, prickly pear slices, a lime wedge and a maraschino cherry. Serve with a couple of drinking straws.

# Mai Tai

A very refreshing, but strong, party drink that slips down easily; just before you do!

### Serves 1

INGREDIENTS
1 measure/22.5 ml/1$^1$/$_2$ tbsp
  white rum
1 measure/22.5 ml/1$^1$/$_2$ tbsp dark
  rum
1 measure/22.5 ml/1$^1$/$_2$ tbsp
  apricot brandy
3 measures/70 ml/4$^1$/$_2$ tbsp
  orange juice, chilled
3 measures/70 ml/4$^1$/$_2$ tbsp
  pineapple juice, chilled
1 measure/22.5 ml/1$^1$/$_2$ tbsp
  grenadine

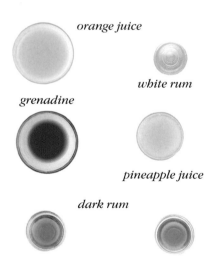

*orange juice*

*grenadine*

*white rum*

*pineapple juice*

*dark rum*

*apricot brandy*

## VARIATION
Mix bitters, rum, orgeat (almond and orange flower water) syrup or almond essence into 300ml (10 fl oz) orange juice.

**1** Add the white and dark rum and apricot brandy to a cocktail shaker half-full of cracked ice.

**2** Add the well chilled orange and pineapple juices.

**3** Shake together well for about 20 seconds, or until the outside of the cocktail shaker feels cold. Strain into a tumbler of ice.

**4** Slowly pour the grenadine into the glass and it will fall to the bottom of the drink to make a glowing red layer.

# Morning Glory Fizz

A good early-morning drink, which should be consumed as soon as it is made, before it loses its flavour and bubbles.

## Serves 1

INGREDIENTS
2/3 measure/15 ml/1 tbsp brandy
1/4 measure/5 ml/1 tsp orange
   curaçao
1/4 measure/5 ml/1 tsp lemon
   juice
1 dash anisette
2 dashes angostura bitters
soda water, to taste
twist of lemon rind, to decorate

*anisette*

*brandy*

*orange curaçao*

*angostura bitters*

*lemon juice*

*soda water*

*lemon rind*

**1** Pour the brandy, curaçao, lemon juice and anisette into a cocktail shaker containing ice and shake for 20 seconds.

**2** Strain the drink into a small chilled cocktail glass.

**3** Add the angostura bitters to taste and top up with soda water.

**4** Using a canelle knife cut a long thin piece of lemon rind. Curl the lemon rind into a tight coil and add to the drink.

## VARIATION

Shake together an egg white, sugar syrup to taste, the juice of 1/2 lemon and 1/2 lime and gin or whisky instead of the brandy and add a splash of Chartreuse. Shake well and top up with soda.

# Cider Cup

Cups make an excellent long and refreshing drink for an apéritif or party. Mix up just before serving.

## Serves 6

INGREDIENTS
rind of 1 lemon
slices of orange
5 measures/120 ml/4 fl oz pale
   sherry
3 measures/70 ml/4$\frac{1}{2}$ tbsp brandy
   or clove brandy
3 measures/70 ml/4$\frac{1}{2}$ tbsp white
   curaçao
2 measures/45 ml/3 tbsp amaretto
600 ml/20 fl oz good quality
   medium sweet cider
cucumber, to decorate

*cucumber peel*

*amaretto*

*orange slices*

*lemon rind*

*medium sweet cider*

*pale sherry*

*white curaçao*

*brandy*

**1** Partly fill a jug with cracked ice and add the lemon rind and orange slices.

**2** Add the sherry, brandy, curaçao and amaretto to the ice and stir well to mix.

**3** Pour in the cider and stir gently with a long swizzle stick.

**4** Using a canelle knife, peel the cucumber around in a continuous piece, to produce a spiral. Serve the cocktail in chilled glasses, decorated with the fruit and a twist of cucumber peel.

## VARIATION

Instead of brandy, use Calvados for a richer flavour and add a little maraschino cherry juice to give more colour.

# Havana Cobbler

A very old-fashioned drink that is surprisingly refreshing served in hot weather.

## Serves 1

INGREDIENTS
5 ml/1 tsp sugar syrup
$^1/_2$ measure/10 ml/2 tsp green
    ginger wine
1 measure/22.5 ml/1$^1/_2$ tbsp
    Cuban or white rum
1 measure/22.5 ml/1$^1/_2$ tbsp port

*white rum*

*sugar syrup*

*ginger wine*

*port*

## VARIATION

Cobblers can be made with brandy, gin and sherry and even wine or champagne; for the latter, naturally, don't shake it and omit the port!

**1** Put the sugar syrup and ginger wine in a cocktail shaker, half-filled with ice. Add the white rum.

**2** Shake together for 20 seconds.

**3** Strain the cocktail into a chilled short tumbler.

**4** Tilt the glass and slowly pour the port down the side of the glass to form a layer floating on top of the cocktail.

# Moscow Mule

One of the classic American vodka-based cocktails, which uses a large quantity of angostura bitters for its flavour and colour and enough vodka to give the drink a real kick.

## Serves 1

INGREDIENTS
2 measures/45 ml/3 tbsp vodka
6 dashes angostura bitters
dash lime cordial
$^1/_2$ measure/10 ml/2 tsp lime juice
3 measures/70 ml/4$^1/_2$ tbsp
    ginger beer
slices of lime, to decorate

angostura bitters

lime slices

lime juice

vodka

lime cordial

ginger beer

**1** Pour the vodka, bitters, lime cordial and lime juice into a bar glass of ice. Mix together well.

**2** Strain into a tumbler containing a couple of ice cubes.

**3** Top up the mixture, to taste, with ginger beer.

**4** Add a few halved slices of lime to the cocktail before serving.

## VARIATION

For a Malawi Shandy, mix ice-cold ginger beer with a dash of bitters and top up with soda water. Of course, the vodka does not have to be left out.

# Vodka and Kumquat Lemonade

A mild-sounding name for a strong concoction of kumquat and peppercorn-flavoured vodka and white curaçao.

## VARIATION

Use elderflower or fruit cordial, with gin or vodka as the base, and top up with soda or tonic water.

## Serves 2

INGREDIENTS
75g/3 oz kumquats
5 measures/120 ml/4 fl oz vodka
3 black peppercorns, cracked (optional)
²/₃ measure/15 ml/1 tbsp white curaçao or orange syrup
²/₃ measure/15 ml/1 tbsp lemon juice
7 measures/150 ml/5 fl oz mineral or soda water
sprigs of mint, to decorate

*white curaçao*

*kumquats*

*sprig of mint*

*lemon juice*

*black peppercorns*

*soda water*

*vodka*

**1** Slice the kumquats thickly and add to the vodka in an airtight jar with the cracked black peppercorns, if using. Leave aside for a couple of hours, overnight or up to a month.

**2** Fill a jug with cracked ice and then add the curaçao or orange syrup, the lemon juice and the kumquat-flavoured vodka with the sliced kumquats.

**3** Using a long swizzle stick, mix together well.

**4** Add the mineral or soda water and a few fresh mint leaves and gently stir everything together.

**5** Pour the drink (lemonade) into chilled glasses of ice.

**6** Add slices of vodka-soaked kumquats to the glasses and decorate with more mint sprigs.

# Horse's Fall

A long drink to serve on a hot summer's day. The addition of strongly-flavoured tea is a matter of taste and preference.

### VARIATION
Substitute calvados or brandy for the flavoured tea for a Horse's Neck.

*Serves 1*

INGREDIENTS
1 lemon
dash angostura bitters
2 measures/45 ml/3 tbsp
   raspberry, Orange Pekoe or
   Assam tea, chilled (optional)
1 measure/22.5 ml/1½ tbsp clear,
   unsweetened apple juice
5 measures/120 ml/4 fl oz dry
   ginger ale or lemonade

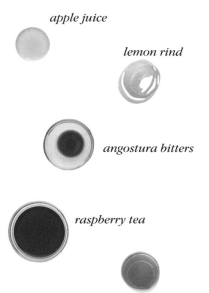

*apple juice*

*lemon rind*

*angostura bitters*

*raspberry tea*

*dry ginger ale*

**1**   Cut the peel from the lemon in one continuous strip and use to line and decorate a long cocktail glass. Chill the glass until required.

**2**   Add a dash of angostura bitters to the bottom of the glass.

**3**   Measure the tea, if using, into the cocktail shaker and add the apple juice.

**4**   Shake everything together for about 20 seconds.

**5**   Strain into the prepared, chilled cocktail glass.

**6**   Top up with chilled ginger ale or lemonade to taste.

# Sunburst

Bursting with freshness and vitamins, this drink is a good early morning pick-me-up.

## Serves 2

INGREDIENTS
1 green apple, cored and chopped
3 carrots, peeled and chopped
1 mango, peeled and stoned
7 measures/150 ml/5 fl oz freshly squeezed orange juice, chilled
6 strawberries, hulled
slice of orange, to decorate

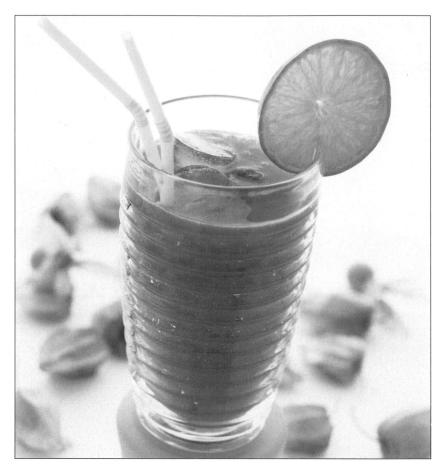

*mango*

*orange juice*

*slice of orange*

*carrots*

*green apple*

*strawberries*

1 Place the apple, carrots and mango in a blender or food processor and process to a pulp.

2 Add the orange juice and strawberries and process again.

3 If liked, strain well through a sieve, pressing out all the juice with the back of a wooden spoon. Discard any pulp left in the sieve.

4 Pour into tumblers filled with ice cubes and serve immediately, decorated with a slice of orange.

## VARIATION

Any combination of fruit juice and yogurt can be shaken together. Try natural yogurt with apple, apricot and mango.

# Scarlet Lady

This drink could fool a few on the first sip, with its fruity and fresh tones. It could easily pass as an alcoholic wine-based cocktail.

## Serves 1

INGREDIENTS
115 g/4 oz Galia, honeydew or
   watermelon
5 small red grapes
3 measures/70 ml/4¹/₂ tbsp
   unsweetened red grape juice

TO DECORATE
red grapes, sugar-frosted
1 egg white, lightly beaten
15 g/¹/₂ oz caster sugar

*red grape juice*

*egg white*

*melon*

*caster sugar*

 *red grapes*

**1** Put the melon and grapes in a blender and process until they form a smooth purée.

**2** Add the red grape juice and continue to process for another minute.

**3** Strain the juice into a bar glass of ice and stir until chilled.

**4** Pour into a chilled cocktail glass and decorate with sugar-frosted grapes threaded on to a cocktail stick.

## VARIATION

For a longer fizzy drink, top up the melon and grape purée with equal quantities of grape juice and tonic or soda water.

# Virgin Prairie Oyster

A superior pick-me-up and a variation on the
Bloody and Virgin Mary. The tomato base can be
drunk without the raw egg yolk, if it does not
appeal to you. Use only fresh free-range eggs.

## Serves 1

INGREDIENTS
175 ml/6 fl oz tomato juice
10 ml/2 tsp Worcestershire sauce
5–10 ml/1–2 tsp balsamic vinegar
1 egg yolk
cayenne pepper, to taste

balsamic
vinegar

tomato juice

egg yolk

Worcestershire
sauce

cayenne pepper

## VARIATION

Shake together equal quantities of
fresh grapefruit juice and tomato
juice, with a dash of Worcestershire
sauce. Strain into a tall and narrow
highball glass.

**1** Measure the tomato juice into a
large bar glass and stir over plenty of ice,
until well chilled.

**2** Strain into a tall tumbler half-filled
with ice cubes.

**3** Add the Worcestershire sauce and
balsamic vinegar, to taste, and use a
swizzle stick to mix together.

**4** Float the egg yolk on top and lightly
dust with cayenne pepper.

# Fruit and Ginger Ale

An old English mulled drink, served chilled over ice. Of course it can be made with ready-squeezed apple and orange juices, but roasting the fruit with cloves gives a much better flavour.

## Serves 4–6

INGREDIENTS
1 cooking apple
1 orange, scrubbed
1 lemon, scrubbed
20 whole cloves
7.5 cm/3 in fresh root ginger, peeled
25 g/1 oz soft brown sugar
350 ml/12 fl oz bitter lemon or non-alcoholic wine
wedges of orange rind and whole cloves, to decorate

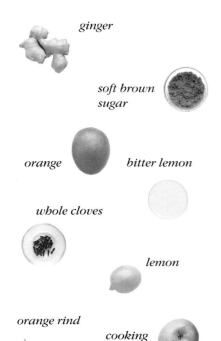

*ginger*

*soft brown sugar*

*orange*          *bitter lemon*

*whole cloves*

*lemon*

*orange rind*

*cooking apple*

**1** Preheat the oven to 200°C/400°F/ Gas 6. Score the apple around the middle and stud the orange and lemon with the cloves. Bake them in the oven for 25 minutes until soft and completely cooked through.

**2** Quarter the orange and lemon and pulp the apple, discarding the skin and the core. Finely grate the ginger. Place the fruit and ginger together in a bowl with the soft brown sugar.

**3** Add 300 ml/10 fl oz boiling water. Using a spoon, squeeze the fruit to release more flavour. Cover and leave to cool for an hour or overnight.

**4** Strain into a jug of cracked ice and use a spoon to press out all the juices from the fruit. Add the bitter lemon or non-alcoholic wine, to taste. Decorate with orange rind and cloves.

# Blushing Piña Colada

This is good with or without the rum. Don't be tempted to put roughly crushed ice into the blender; it will not be as smooth and will ruin the blades. Make sure you crush it well first.

## VARIATION

For classic Piña Colada use vanilla ice cream and 1 measure white rum. For a Passionate Encounter, blend 2 scoops passion fruit sorbet and 15 ml/1 tbsp coconut milk with a measure each of pineapple and apricot juice.

## Serves 2

INGREDIENTS

1 banana, peeled and sliced
1 thick slice pineapple, peeled
3 measures/70 ml/4¹/₂ tbsp
    pineapple juice
1 scoop strawberry ice cream or
    sorbet
1 measure/22.5 ml/1¹/₂ tbsp
    coconut milk
30 ml/2 tbsp grenadine
wedges of pineapple and stemmed
    maraschino cherries, to decorate

*coconut milk*

*slice of pineapple*

*pineapple juice*

*grenadine*

*maraschino cherry*

*strawberry ice cream*

*banana*

**1**  Roughly chop the banana. Cut two small wedges from the pineapple for decoration and reserve. Cut up the remainder of the pineapple and add to the blender with the banana.

**2**  Add the pineapple juice to the blender and process until the mixture is a smooth purée.

**3**  Add the strawberry ice cream or sorbet with the coconut milk and a small scoop of finely crushed ice, and process until smooth.

**4**  Pour into two large, well-chilled cocktail glasses.

**5**  Pour the grenadine syrup slowly on top of the Piña Colada; it will filter through the drink in a dappled effect.

**6**  Decorate each glass with a wedge of pineapple and a stemmed cherry and serve with drinking straws.

# Volunteer

This is an ideal pick-me-up or non-alcoholic drink for the chosen driver at a party. It was devised and drunk during a very rough channel crossing in too small a boat!

## *Serves 1*

INGREDIENTS
2 measures/45 ml/3 tbsp lime
   cordial
2–3 dashes angostura bitters
7 measures/150 ml/5 fl oz chilled
   tonic water
frozen slices of lime, to decorate
decorative ice cubes, to serve

*tonic water*

*angostura bitters*

*lime cordial*

*frozen slices of lime*

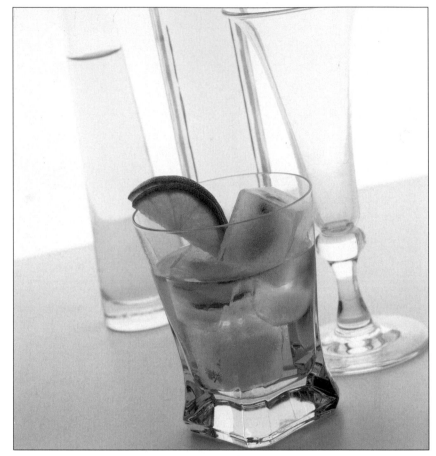

**1** Place the lime cordial at the bottom of the glass and shake in the angostura bitters, according to taste.

**2** Add a few decorative ice cubes to the glass, if liked.

**3** Top up with tonic water and add the frozen lime slices.

## VARIATION
Use fresh lime or grapefruit juice and a splash of sugar syrup instead of the lime cordial, and top up with ginger ale.

# Steel Works

A thirst quenching drink, which is ideal to serve at any time of the day or night.

## Serves 1

INGREDIENTS
2 measures/45 ml/3 tbsp passion-
    fruit cordial
dash angostura bitters
3 measures/70 ml/4½ tbsp soda
    water, chilled
3 measures/70 ml/4½ tbsp
    lemonade, chilled
1 passion fruit, (optional)

*lemonade*

*passion-fruit
cordial*

*passion fruit*

*soda water*

*angostura bitters*

**1** Pour the passion-fruit cordial straight into a long tumbler. Add the angostura bitters to the glass and then add some ice cubes.

**2** Top up the drink with the chilled soda water and lemonade and stir briefly together.

**3** Cut the passion fruit in half, if using; scoop the seeds and flesh from the fruit and add to the drink. Stir the drink gently before serving.

## VARIATION

For a Rock Shandy, pour equal quantities of lemonade and soda on to bitters or use your favourite variety of the naturally flavoured and unsweetened fruit cordials.

# Bandrek

A rich and creamy version of the spicy Indonesian drink. Serve warm or chilled. If you like, add a very fresh egg to the syrup and milks in the blender and you'll have an egg-nog.

## VARIATION

Stir ¹/₂ measure/10 ml/2 tsp whisky into the finished drink or add the strained spiced syrup to double-strength black coffee. Process in a blender with a little double cream, strain and serve over ice.

## Serves 1

INGREDIENTS
3 whole cloves
3 juniper berries, bruised
cinnamon stick
6 green cardamom pods, bruised
4 whole black peppercorns
1 sugar cube
175 ml/6 fl oz water
2 measures/45 ml/3 tbsp
    coconut milk
3 measures/70 ml/4¹/₂ tbsp
    whole milk
cinnamon sticks and a maraschino
    cherry, to decorate

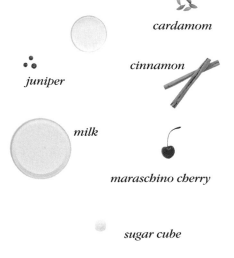

coconut milk

cardamom

cinnamon

juniper

milk

maraschino cherry

sugar cube

**1** Put the cloves, juniper berries, cinnamon, cardamom pods and peppercorns, with the sugar cube, in a saucepan. Heat gently to release the aroma and flavours of the spices.

**2** Add the 175 ml/6 fl oz water and bring to the boil.

**3** Continue to boil for 10 minutes or until reduced to 30–45 ml/2–3 tbsp of spicy flavoured syrup. Remove from the heat and cool.

**4** Pour the syrup into a blender with the coconut milk and whole milk and process until smooth.

**5** Strain over cracked ice into a stemmed glass.

**6** Decorate with cinnamon sticks and a maraschino cherry.

# St Clements

Oranges and lemons create a simple but thirst-quenching drink which confirms that freshly-squeezed fruit has a superior flavour to any other kind that can be bought.

## VARIATION

This same principle can be used to make pineapple, peach, grape and soft fruit juices, but sweeten with sugar syrup. These will keep in the fridge for 2–3 days.

### Serves 1

INGREDIENTS
rind and juice of 2 oranges
rind and juice of 1 lemon
15g/½ oz caster sugar, or to taste
75 ml/5 tbsp water
slices of orange and lemon, to
    decorate

*oranges*

*caster sugar*

*lemon*

*orange and
lemon slices*

**1** Wash the oranges and lemons and then thinly pare off the rind from the fruit with a sharp knife, leaving the white pith behind. Remove the pith from the fruit and discard it.

**2** Put the orange and lemon rind in a saucepan, with the sugar and water. Heat gently over a low heat and stir gently until the sugar has dissolved.

**3** Remove the pan from the heat and press the orange and lemon rind against the sides of the pan to release all their oils. Cover the pan and cool. Remove and discard the rind.

**4** Purée the oranges and lemon and sweeten the fruit pulp by adding the cooled citrus syrup over the fruit pulp. Leave aside for 2–3 hours for the flavours to infuse.

**5** Sieve the fruit pulp, pressing the solids in the sieve to extract as much of the juice as possible.

**6** Pour into a tall glass filled with finely crushed ice and decorate with a slice of orange and lemon.

# Dickson's Bloody Mary

This recipe has plenty of character, with the horseradish, sherry and Tabasco. The true Bloody Mary is a simpler version.

## VARIATION

Use tequila in the place of the vodka for a Bloody Maria and use a clam juice and tomato juice mixture for a Bloody Muddle.

### Serves 1

INGREDIENTS
2 measures/45 ml/3 tbsp vodka or chilli-flavoured vodka
1 measure/22.5 ml/1½ tbsp *fino* sherry
7 measures/150 ml/5 fl oz tomato juice
1 measure/22.5 ml/1½ tbsp lemon juice
10–15 ml/2–3 tsp Worcestershire sauce
2–3 dashes Tabasco sauce
2.5 ml/½ tsp creamed horseradish relish
5 ml/1 tsp celery salt
salt and ground black pepper
celery stick, stuffed green olives, cherry tomato, to decorate

celery

vodka

celery salt

tomato juice

fino sherry

lemon juice

Tabasco sauce

salt and pepper

Worcestershire sauce

creamed horseradish relish

**1** Fill a bar glass or jug with cracked ice and add the vodka, sherry and tomato juice. Stir well.

**2** Add the lemon juice, Worcestershire and Tabasco sauces and the horseradish, according to taste.

**3** Add the celery salt, salt and pepper and stir until the glass has frosted and the Bloody Mary is chilled.

**4** Strain into a long tumbler, half-filled with a couple of ice cubes.

**5** Add a decorative stick of celery as a swizzle stick.

**6** Finish off the cocktail by threading a cocktail stick with olives and a cherry tomato, and add to the rim of the glass.

# Apricot Bellini

This is a version of the famous apéritif served at Harry's Bar in Venice. Instead of the usual peaches and peach brandy, apricot nectar and apricot brandy make this a tempting variation.

## VARIATION

Instead of apricots and apricot brandy, use fresh raspberries and raspberry-infused gin or syrup.

## Serves 6–8

INGREDIENTS
3 apricots
10 ml/2 tsp lemon juice
10 ml/2 tsp sugar syrup
2 measures/45 ml/3 tbsp apricot
　brandy or peach schnapps
1 bottle *brut* champagne or dry
　sparkling wine, chilled

*lemon juice*

*apricots*

*sparkling wine*

*apricot brandy*

*sugar syrup*

**1** Plunge the apricots into boiling water for 2 minutes, to loosen the skins.

**2** Peel off the skins of the apricots, remove the stones and discard both.

**3** Process the apricot flesh with the lemon juice until you have a smooth purée. Sweeten to taste with sugar syrup, then sieve.

**4** Add the brandy or peach schnapps to the apricot nectar and mix together.

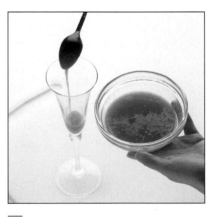

**5** Divide the apricot nectar between the chilled champagne flutes.

**6** Top up the glasses with chilled champagne or sparkling wine.

# Kir Lethale

The raisins for this cocktail can be soaked overnight in vodka.

## *Serves 6*

INGREDIENTS
6 vodka-soaked raisins
30 ml/2 tbsp vodka or
 raisin vodka
3 measures/70 ml/4$^1$/$_2$ tbsp
 crème de cassis
1 bottle *brut* champagne or dry
 sparkling wine, chilled

crème de cassis

vodka-soaked raisins

champagne

## VARIATION

For Kir Framboise, use crème de framboise or raspberry syrup and raspberry-flavoured vodka.

**1** Place a vodka-soaked raisin at the bottom of each glass.

**2** Add a teaspoon of vodka or the vodka from the steeped raisins, if using, to each glass.

**3** Divide the crème de cassis equally between the glasses.

**4** Only when ready to serve, top up each glass with the champagne or dry sparkling wine.

# Brandy Blazer

A warming after-dinner tipple, ideal served with fresh vanilla ice cream or caramelized oranges.

## Serves 1

**INGREDIENTS**
½ orange
1 lemon
2 measures/45 ml/3 tbsp cognac
1 sugar cube
½ measure/10 ml/2 tsp Kahlúa
pieces of orange rind, threaded
    on to a cocktail stick, to decorate

*lemon*

*orange rind decoration*

*Kahlúa*

*orange*

*cognac*

*sugar cube*

## VARIATION
Pour the hot cognac and Kahlúa mix on to freshly brewed coffee and serve black.

**1** Thinly pare the rind from the orange and lemon, removing and discarding as much of the white pith as possible.

**2** Put the cognac, sugar cube, lemon and orange rind in a small pan.

**3** Heat gently, then remove from the heat, light a match and pass the flame close to the surface of the liquid. The alcohol will burn with a low, blue flame for about a minute. Blow out the flame.

**4** Add the Kahlúa to the pan and strain into a heat resistant liqueur glass and decorate with the cocktail stick threaded with orange rind. Serve warm.

# Long Island Iced Tea

A long, potent drink that has an intoxicating effect, which is well disguised by the cola. For a simpler version, use equal quantities of rum, Cointreau, tequila and lemon juice and top up with cola.

## Serves 1

INGREDIENTS

¹/₂ measure/10 ml/2 tsp white rum
¹/₂ measure/10 ml/2 tsp vodka
¹/₂ measure/10 ml/2 tsp gin
¹/₂ measure/10 ml/2 tsp Grand
    Marnier or Cointreau
1 measure/22.5 ml/1¹/₂ tbsp cold
    Earl Grey tea
juice ¹/₂ lemon
cola, chilled, to taste
slices of lemon and a large sprig
    of mint, to decorate

*Grand Marnier*

*gin*

*Earl Grey tea*

*white rum*

*vodka*

*lemon juice*

*cola*

*lemon slices*

*mint*

**1**  Fill a bar glass with cracked ice and add the rum, vodka, gin and Grand Marnier or Cointreau.

**2**  Add the cold Earl Grey tea to the spirits in the bar glass.

**3**  Stir well for 30 seconds to chill the spirits and the tea.

**4**  Add the lemon juice, to taste.

**5**  Strain into a highball tumbler filled with ice cubes and lemon slices.

**6**  Add the chilled cola, according to taste, and add a sprig of fresh mint to use as a swizzle stick.

# Mint Julep

One of the oldest cocktails, this originated in the southern States of America. Add fresh mint leaves according to taste.

## VARIATION

Add a dash of chilled soda for a refreshing long drink.

### *Serves 1*

**INGREDIENTS**
15 ml/1 tbsp caster sugar
8–10 fresh mint leaves
15 ml/1 tbsp hot water
2 measures/45 ml/3 tbsp bourbon
   or whisky

*hot water*

*mint leaves*

*caster sugar*

*bourbon*

**1** Place the sugar in a pestle and mortar, or in a bar glass with a muddler. Tear the mint leaves into small pieces and add to the sugar.

**2** Bruise the mint leaves to release their flavour and colour.

**3** Add the hot water to the mint leaves and grind well together.

**4** Spoon into a snifter glass or brandy balloon and half fill with crushed ice.

**5** Add the bourbon or whisky to the snifter glass.

**6** Stir until the outside of the glass has frosted. Allow to stand for a couple of minutes, to let the ice melt slightly and dilute the drink. Serve with straws, if liked.

# Frozen Strawberry Daiquiri

A version of the Cuban original, which was made only with local Cuban rum, lime juice and sugar. When out of season, use drained, canned strawberries instead.

### VARIATION
Substitute 50 ml/2 fl oz cream for the rum and brandy. Process together in the blender and serve as a non-alcoholic daiquiri.

## Serves 1

INGREDIENTS
4 whole strawberries
10 ml/2 tsp lime juice
1 measure/22.5 ml/1¹/₂ tbsp brandy
   or strawberry brandy
1 measure/22.5 ml/1¹/₂ tbsp
   white rum
dash of grenadine
strawberry and a sprig of mint, to
   decorate

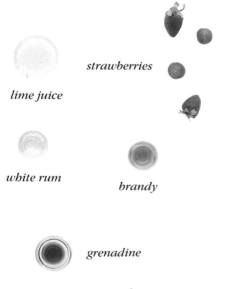

*strawberries*

*lime juice*

*white rum*

*brandy*

*grenadine*

*sprig of
mint*

**1** Place ice cubes in a clean, folded tea towel and crush to a fine snow, using a rolling pin or hammer.

**2** Place the strawberries with the lime juice and brandy in a blender and process to a purée.

**3** Add the white rum, grenadine and half a glass of finely crushed ice to the blender and process once more, to a smooth slush.

**4** Pour the mixture into a well-chilled cocktail glass.

**5** To decorate, remove the hull from the strawberry and replace with a small sprig of fresh mint.

**6** Make a cut in the side of the strawberry and attach to the rim of the glass. Serve with a short straw, if liked.

# Wilga Hill Boomerang

This sundowner is mixed in a large bar glass half-full of ice cubes, and is served super cold.

## Serves 1

INGREDIENTS
1 measure/22.5 ml/1$\frac{1}{2}$ tbsp gin
$\frac{1}{4}$ measure/5 ml/1 tsp dry
    vermouth
$\frac{1}{4}$ measure/5 ml/1 tsp sweet
    vermouth
1 measure/22.5 ml/1$\frac{1}{2}$ tbsp clear
    apple juice
dash angostura bitters
2 dashes maraschino cherry juice
strip of orange rind and a
    maraschino cherry, to decorate

*orange rind*

*clear apple juice*

*dry vermouth*

*angostura bitters*

*maraschino cherry and juice*

*gin*

*sweet vermouth*

## VARIATION

Drop the apple juice and serve over the rocks or, if liked, substitute bourbon or Southern Comfort for the gin.

**1** Pour the gin, dry and sweet vermouths and apple juice into a bar glass half filled with ice, and stir until the outside of the glass has frosted.

**2** Add the angostura bitters and maraschino juice to the bottom of a cocktail glass and add ice cubes.

**3** Strain the gin and vermouths into a shorts tumbler.

**4** Add the strip of orange rind and a maraschino cherry and serve.

# Golden Start

A delicious and very drinkable mix of Galliano, orange, pineapple and coconut cream.

### Serves 1

INGREDIENTS
2 measures/45 ml/3 tbsp Galliano
1 measure/22.5 ml/1½ tbsp
  orange juice, chilled
1 measure/22.5 ml/1½ tbsp
  pineapple juice, chilled
1 measure/22.5 ml/1½ tbsp
  white or orange curaçao
1 measure/22.5 ml/1½ tbsp
  coconut cream
30 ml/2 tbsp pineapple juice, to
  decorate
25 g/1 oz caster sugar, to
  decorate

*white curaçao*   *Galliano*

*caster sugar*

*orange juice*

*pineapple juice*

*coconut cream*

## VARIATION

Substitute light crème de cacao for the curaçao, to give that extra tropical twist.

**1** Put the Galliano, orange and pineapple juices and curaçao in a blender and process together.

**2** Add the coconut cream with a tablespoon of fine ice snow and process until smooth and frothy.

**3** Rub the rim of the cocktail glass with pineapple juice and invert the glass into a saucer of sugar, to frost the rim.

**4** Pour the cocktail into the prepared glass while still frothy.

# Sea Dog

A long whisky drink with a citrus twist. For a sweeter drink, add a second sugar lump; if including Drambuie, only use one.

## VARIATION

Use gin in place of the whisky and Pimms in place of the Benedictine.

### Serves 1

INGREDIENTS
1–2 sugar cubes
2 dashes angostura bitters
2 orange wedges
2 lemon wedges
$^2/_3$ measure/15 ml/1 tbsp whisky or
  Drambuie
1 measure/22.5 ml/1$^1/_2$ tbsp
  Benedictine
2 measures/45 ml/2 fl oz/3 tbsp
  soda water, chilled
maraschino cherry, to decorate

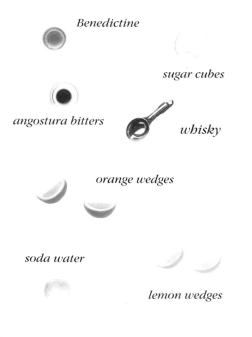

*Benedictine*

*sugar cubes*

*angostura bitters*

*whisky*

*orange wedges*

*soda water*

*lemon wedges*

*maraschino cherry*

**1** Put the sugar cube at the bottom of a Collins glass, add the bitters and allow to soak into the sugar cube.

**2** Add the orange and lemon wedges and, using a muddler, press the juices from the fruit.

**3** Fill the glass with cracked ice.

**4** Add the whisky and the Benedictine and mix together well with a swizzle stick for 20 seconds.

**5** Top up with chilled soda water.

**6** Serve with the muddler, so that more juice can be pressed from the fruit, according to personal taste; decorate with a maraschino cherry.

# Harvey Wallbanger

The next step on from a Screwdriver – add a dash of Galliano. Those who like a stronger version should add an extra measure of vodka.

**VARIATION**

Mix together the orange juice and vodka with a splash of ginger wine, pour into a glass and slowly pour the Galliano on top.

## Serves 1

INGREDIENTS
1 measure/22.5 ml/1½ tbsp vodka
⅔ measure/15 ml/1 tbsp Galliano
7 measures/150 ml/5 fl oz
    orange juice
½ small orange, to decorate

*orange juice*

*Galliano*

*orange*

*vodka*

**1** Pour the vodka, Galliano and orange juice into a bar glass of ice.

**2** Mix the cocktail and ice for 30 seconds, to chill it well.

**3** Using a canelle knife, take a series of strips of rind off the orange, running from the top to the bottom of the fruit.

**4** Use a small sharp knife to cut the orange evenly and thinly into slices.

**5** Cut the orange slices in half and wedge them between cracked ice in a highball glass.

**6** Strain the chilled cocktail into the prepared glass.

# Apple Sour

For those with concerns about eating raw egg, this variation on a Brandy Sour can be made without the egg white. Applejack or apple schnapps also work well, in place of the calvados.

## Serves 1

INGREDIENTS
1 measure/22.5 ml/1¹⁄₂ tbsp
  calvados
²⁄₃ measure/15 ml/1 tbsp lemon
  juice
5 ml/1 tsp caster sugar
dash angostura bitters
1 egg white
red and green apple slices and
  lemon juice, to decorate

*egg white*

*lemon juice*

*caster sugar*

*angostura bitters*

*red and green apples*

*calvados*

**I** Put the calvados, lemon juice and caster sugar into a shaker of ice, with the angostura bitters and egg white.

**2** Shake together for 30 seconds.

**3** Strain the cocktail into a tumbler of cracked ice.

**4** Dip the red and green apple slices in lemon juice. Decorate the cocktail with the apple slices threaded on to a bamboo skewer.

## VARIATION

Sours can also be made with Amaretto or tequila; add a splash of raspberry syrup or port to the glass just before serving.

# East India

This short and elegant drink can be served as an apéritif, dressed with a twist of lime rind and a maraschino cherry.

## Serves 1

INGREDIENTS
²/₃ measure/15 ml/1 tbsp brandy
2 dashes white curaçao
2 dashes pineapple juice
2 dashes angostura bitters
1 lime and a maraschino cherry, to decorate

*maraschino cherry*

*lime*

*angostura bitters*

*white curaçao*

*brandy*

*pineapple juice*

## VARIATION

Mix equal quantities of dry vermouth and dry sherry with angostura bitters and serve on the rocks.

**1** Put the brandy, curaçao, pineapple juice and bitters into a bar glass of ice.

**2** Stir the cocktail well for about 20 seconds until chilled and strain into a squat tumbler over the rocks.

**3** Using a canelle knife, remove a piece of rind from a lime.

**4** Tightly twist into a coil, hold for a few seconds, and add to the drink with a maraschino cherry.

# Planters Punch

This long refreshing old colonial drink originates from the sugar plantations found throughout the West Indies.

VARIATION
Add 1 measure/22.5 ml/1½ tbsp cold Assam tea, for a different tang.

## Serves 1

INGREDIENTS
1 measure/22.5 ml/1½ tbsp lime juice
1 measure/22.5 ml/1½ tbsp orange juice (optional)
2 measures/45 ml/3 tbsp dark rum
10 ml/2 tsp grenadine
dash angostura bitters
soda water or lemonade, chilled
peach slices and a Cape gooseberry, to decorate

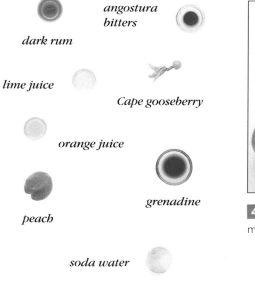

*dark rum*

*angostura bitters*

*lime juice*

*Cape gooseberry*

*orange juice*

*grenadine*

*peach*

*soda water*

**1** Squeeze the lime and orange juices and add to a bar glass of ice.

**2** Add the dark rum and the grenadine and mix together for about 20 seconds.

**3** Add a dash of bitters to the bottom of a tumbler of decorative ice cubes.

**4** Strain the rum and grenadine mixture into the chilled tumbler.

**5** Top up with plenty of chilled soda water or lemonade.

**6** Decorate with peach slices and a Cape gooseberry.

# Singapore Sling

The origins of this old-fashioned thirst quencher lie far away to the east.

## Serves 1

INGREDIENTS
2 measures/45 ml/3 tbsp gin
juice 1 lemon
5 ml/1 tsp caster sugar
soda water, chilled
2/3 measure/15 ml/1 tbsp Cointreau
2/3 measure/15 ml/1 tbsp cherry
    brandy
1 lemon, to decorate
black cherry, to decorate

*black cherry*

*lemon*

*gin*

*Cointreau*

*cherry brandy*

*caster sugar*

*soda water*

### VARIATION
Substitute Bénédictine for the Cointreau for a Straits Sling, and add ginger beer instead of soda water for a Raffles Bar Sling.

**1** Pour the gin into a bar glass of ice and mix with the lemon juice and sugar.

**2** Strain the cocktail into a tumbler full of cracked ice.

**3** Top up the cocktail with chilled soda water, to taste.

**4** Add the Cointreau and the cherry brandy, but do not stir.

**5** To decorate, use a vegetable peeler or sharp knife to cut a long piece of rind round and round the lemon.

**6** Arrange the lemon rind in the glass. Thread the cherry on to two cocktail sticks and add to the rim of the glass.

# Kew Pimms

A very drinkable concoction of sweet vermouth, curaçao, vodka, gin and cherry brandy served over summer fruit.

VARIATION
Top up the spirit base with champagne, sparkling wine or tonic water.

## Serves 1

INGREDIENTS

1 measure/22.5 ml/1¹/₂ tbsp sweet vermouth

1 measure/22.5 ml/1¹/₂ tbsp orange curaçao

²/₃ measure/15 ml/1 tbsp vodka

²/₃ measure/15 ml/1 tbsp gin

²/₃ measure/15 ml/1 tbsp cherry brandy

assorted soft summer fruits

1–2 dashes angostura bitters

2 measures/45 ml/3 tbsp American dry ginger ale, chilled

2 measures/45 ml/3 tbsp lemonade, chilled

1 lemon, to decorate

lemon balm or mint leaves, to decorate

lemon balm

lemon

vodka

orange curaçao

angostura bitters

summer fruits

sweet vermouth    gin

cherry brandy

lemonade

dry ginger ale

**1** Measure the vermouth, curaçao, vodka, gin and cherry brandy into a bar glass of ice and stir well to chill.

**2** Strain into a tall highball tumbler full of ice cubes and soft summer fruits.

**3** Add the bitters and then pour in equal quantities of chilled ginger ale and lemonade to taste.

**4** To make the lemon triangles, pare a thin piece of lemon rind from the lemon.

**5** Cut the rind into a rectangle and cut a slit three-quarters of the way across the lemon rind. Turn the rectangle and repeat from the other side.

**6** Twist to form a triangle, crossing the ends to secure. Add to the drink with lemon balm or mint leaves.

INDEX

**A**

Airstrike, 36
Amaretto, 10, 30, 50
angostura bitters, 13
  Apple Sour, 88
  Bitter Gimlet, 31
  East India, 89
  Gall Bracer, 24
  Gin Crusta, 34
  Horse's Fall, 56
  Kew Pimms, 94
  Moscow Mule, 53
  Planters Punch, 90
  Sea Dog, 84
  Steel Works, 65
  Volunteer, 64
  Vunderful, 44
  Wilga Hill Boomerang, 82
anisette, 10, 49
apple, 58, 61, 88
apple juice, 12, 56, 82
Apple Sour, 88
Apricot Bellini, 72
apricot brandy, 48, 72

**B**

B52, 37
Bailey's Irish Cream, 37
balsamic vinegar, 13, 60
banana, 62
Bandrek, 66
Benedictine, 10, 84
Bitter Gimlet, 31
bitter lemon, 12
Blue Hawaiian, 46
Blushing Piña Colada, 62
bourbon, 78
brandy, 8
  Airstrike, 36
  Brandy Alexander, 26
  Brandy Blazer, 75
  Cider Cup, 50
  Coffee and Chocolate Flip, 38
  Cranberry Kiss, 40
  East India, 89
  Frozen Strawberry
    Daiquiri, 80
  Morning Glory Fizz, 49

**C**

calvados, Apple Sour, 88
carrots, Sunburst, 58
champagne, 8, 72, 74
chartreuse, 10
cherry brandy, 92, 94
Chilli Vodkatini, 32
chilli-vodka, 32, 70
cider, 8, 50
Cider Cup, 50
cider vinegar, 13
coconut cream, 46

coconut milk, 12, 62, 66
Coffee and Chocolate Flip, 38
cognac, Brandy Blazer, 75
Cointreau, 10
  Hooded Claw, 30
  Long-Island Iced Tea, 76
  Margarita, 28
  Singapore Sling, 92
cola, Long-Island Iced Tea, 76
cranberry juice, 12, 40
Cranberry Kiss, 40
cream, Grasshopper, 42
cream liqueurs, 10
crème de cacao, 10, 26, 42
crème de cassis, 10, 43, 74
crème de menthe, 10, 42
curaçao, 10
  Blue Hawaiian, 46
  Cider Cup, 50
  East India, 89
  Kew Pimms, 94
  Morning Glory Fizz, 49
  Vodka & Kumquat
    Lemonade, 54

**D**

Dickson's Bloody Mary, 70
Drambuie, 10, 84

**E**

East India, 89
egg, 38, 60, 88
equipment, 14-15

**F**

flavours, 13
frosting glasses, 19
Frozen Strawberry Daiquiri, 80
Fruit and Ginger Ale, 61

**G**

Gall Bracer, 24
Galliano, 10, 36, 86
garnishes, 17
Gibson, 25
gin, 8
  Bitter Gimlet, 31
  Gibson, 25
  Gin Crusta, 34
  Gin Smash, 22
  Kew Pimms, 94
  Long-Island Iced Tea, 76
  Singapore Sling, 92
  Vunderful, 44
  Wilga Hill Boomerang, 82
ginger ale, 12, 56, 94
ginger beer, 12, 53
ginger wine, 8, 52
glasses, 16
  frosting, 19
Grand Marnier, 10, 37, 76

grape juice, 13, 59
grapefruit juice, 13
grapes, Scarlet Lady, 59
Grasshopper, 42
grenadine, 13
  Blushing Piña Colada, 62
  Frozen Strawberry
    Daiquiri, 80
  Gall Bracer, 24
  Mai Tai, 48
  Planters Punch, 90

**H**

Harvey Wallbanger, 86
Havana Cobbler, 52
herbs, 13
honey, Tequila Sunset, 43
Hooded Claw, 30
Horse's Fall, 56
horseradish relish, 70

**I**

ice: crushing, 18
  decorative cubes, 18
ice cream, 62,

**J**

juices, 12-13

**K**

Kahlúa, 10, 37, 38, 75
Kew Pimms, 94
Kir Lethale, 74
kümmel, 10
kumquat, 54

**L**

lemon: Brandy Blazer, 75
  Fruit and Ginger Ale, 61
  Gin Crusta, 34
  Horse's Fall, 56
  St Clements, 68
lemon juice: Apple Sour, 88
  Apricot Bellini, 72
  Dickson's Bloody Mary, 70
  Morning Glory Fizz, 49
  Singapore Sling, 92
  Tequila Sunset, 43
  Vodka & Kumquat
    Lemonade, 54
lemonade, 12
  Horse's Fall, 56
  Kew Pimms, 94
  Planters Punch, 90
  Steel Works, 65
  Vunderful, 44
lime, Bitter Gimlet, 31
lime cordial, 13, 53, 64
lime juice: Frozen Strawberry
    Daiquiri, 80
  Margarita, 28

Moscow Mule, 53
  Planters Punch, 90
liqueurs, 10
Long-Island Iced Tea, 76
lychees, Vunderful, 44

**M**

Mai Tai, 48
mango, Sunburst, 58
maraschino cherry juice, 34
Margarita, 28
Marsala, 8, 40
mint, 22, 78
Mint Julep, 78
mixers, 12-13
Morning Glory Fizz, 49
Moscow Mule, 53

**O**

orange: Brandy Blazer, 75
  Fruit and Ginger Ale, 61
  St Clements, 68
  Sea Dog, 84
orange juice, 13
  Harvey Wallbanger, 86
  Mai Tai, 48
  Planters Punch, 90
  Sunburst, 58
  Tequila Sunset, 43

**P**

passion fruit cordial, 13, 65
peaches, Vunderful, 44
Perfect Manhattan, 27
Pimms, Vunderful, 44
pineapple juice, 13, 46, 48,
  62, 89
pink grapefruit juice, 13, 40
Planters Punch, 90
port, 8, 52
prune juice, 13, 30

**R**

raisins, Kir Lethale, 74
red grape juice, 13
rum, 8
  Havana Cobbler, 52
  Mai Tai, 48
  Planters Punch, 90
  see also white rum

**S**

St Clements, 68
sauces, 13
Scarlet Lady, 59
schnapps, 8
Sea Dog, 84
shaking cocktails, 19
sherry, 8, 50, 70
Singapore Sling, 92
soda water, 13, 90

Southern Comfort, 10
spices, 13
spirits, 8
  flavoured, 21
  steeping, 21
star anise, Airstrike, 36
Steel Works, 65
strawberries, 58, 80
Sunburst, 58
syrups, 13
  basic, 20
  flavoured, 20

**T**

Tabasco sauce, 70
tea, 56, 76
tequila, 8, 28, 43
Tequila Sunset, 43
Tia Maria, 10
tomato juice, 13, 60, 70
tonic water, 13, 44, 64

**V**

vermouth, 8
  Chilli Vodkatini, 32
  Gibson, 25
  Kew Pimms, 94
  Perfect Manhattan, 27
  Wilga Hill Boomerang, 82
Virgin Prairie Oyster, 60
vodka, 8
  Dickson's Bloody Mary, 70
  Harvey Wallbanger, 86
  Kew Pimms, 94
  Kir Lethale, 74
  Long-Island Iced Tea, 76
  Moscow Mule, 53
  Vodka & Kumquat
    Lemonade, 54
  see also chilli-vodka
Volunteer, 64
Vunderful, 44

**W**

watermelon, Scarlet Lady, 59
whisky, 8
  Gall Bracer, 24
  Mint Julep, 78
  Perfect Manhattan, 27
  Sea Dog, 84
white rum: Blue Hawaiian, 46
  Frozen Strawberry
    Daiquiri, 80
  Long-Island Iced Tea, 76
  Mai Tai, 48
  see also rum
Wilga Hill Boomerang, 82
Worcestershire sauce, 70